SATs Skills

Grammar and Punctuation Workbook

8–9 years

Great Clarendon Street, Oxford, OX2 6DP, United Kingdom

Oxford University Press is a department of the University of Oxford.
It furthers the University's objective of excellence in research, scholarship,
and education by publishing worldwide. Oxford is a registered trade mark
of Oxford University Press in the UK and in certain other countries

Text © Michellejoy Hughes 2016
Illustrations © Oxford University Press 2016

The moral rights of the author have been asserted

First published in 2016

All rights reserved. No part of this publication may be reproduced, stored
in a retrieval system, or transmitted, in any form or by any means, without
the prior permission in writing of Oxford University Press, or as expressly
permitted by law, by licence or under terms agreed with the appropriate
reprographics rights organization. Enquiries concerning reproduction
outside the scope of the above should be sent to the Rights Department,
Oxford University Press, at the address above.

You must not circulate this work in any other form and you must impose
this same condition on any acquirer

British Library Cataloguing in Publication Data
Data available

978-0-19-274559-0

15

Paper used in the production of this book is a natural, recyclable product
made from wood grown in sustainable forests. The manufacturing process
conforms to the environmental regulations of the country of origin.

Printed in China

Acknowledgements

Cover illustrations: Lo Cole
Page make-up: OKS

Although we have made every effort to trace and contact all copyright
holders before publication this has not been possible in all cases. If notified,
the publisher will rectify any errors or omissions at the earliest opportunity.

Links to third party websites are provided by Oxford in good faith and for
information only. Oxford disclaims any responsibility for the materials
contained in any third party website referenced in this work.

The manufacturer's authorised representative in the EU for product safety is
Oxford University Press España S.A. of El Parque Empresarial San Fernando de
Henares, Avenida de Castilla, 2 – 28830 Madrid (www.oup.es/en or product.
safety@oup.com). OUP España S.A. also acts as importer into Spain of
products made by the manufacturer.

Unit 1

Bond SATs Skills Grammar and Punctuation 8–9

A Label each sentence as a command, a question, a statement or an exclamation. [12]

Example: *Get up! command*

1. Where are we going? _____
2. I'm having toast for breakfast. _____
3. Catch the ball! _____
4. That's so funny! _____
5. Why are you laughing? _____
6. Knead the dough for ten minutes. _____
7. I must do my piano practice tonight. _____
8. Ouch! That hurt! _____
9. What time is it? _____
10. Oh, what a lovely day it is! _____
11. I think it is going to rain. _____
12. Give me the pencil. _____

> There are different types of sentences: **commands**, **questions**, **exclamations** and **statements**.
>
> - Put the **verb** at the beginning of the sentence to make a **command**. **Commands** sometimes end with an **exclamation mark** (!).
> - Use a **question** word (such as 'How', 'What', 'Why', 'Where', 'When' and 'Who') at the start of a **question** and a **question mark** (?) at the end.
> - Use an **exclamation mark** (!) to show that your writing is meant to be shocking, funny or angry.
> - Use a **full stop** (.) at the end of all other sentences.

B Add a full stop, question mark or exclamation mark to the end of these sentences. [6]

Example: *You've got to be joking !*

1. We are going on holiday to Cornwall tomorrow _____
2. Mum said that my new bed is being delivered today _____
3. Do you know when Molly is arriving _____
4. Dad told a joke and we were helpless with laughter _____
5. What time are you going out _____
6. Put that down and come over here now _____

18

Unit 1   Bond SATs Skills Grammar and Punctuation 8–9

C Put inverted commas around the words spoken in these sentences. [4]

Example: "Are we going out?" asked Jade.

1 Sit, you naughty dog, the woman said. Sit!
2 The man asked the guard, What time is the next train to Bristol?
3 Would you like to come to our party? the twins asked.
4 I can't see you anywhere, Pip said. Where are you?

> The words people say must have **inverted commas** (" and ") at the beginning and end. The spoken words and the punctuation must be included inside the **inverted commas**. At the end of a speech, use a **comma** if the sentence hasn't finished.

D Underline the proper nouns in these sentences. [4]

Example: *The bus to Cardiff stops at Newport.*

1 Mrs Jones teaches science at Ashford Primary School on Thursday afternoons.
2 "Is Gareth playing with Mrs McCurdy's son, Owen?"
3 Ivanka is moving to Lincoln in October.
4 "I will take Poppy to the vet on Tuesday."

> Always use a capital letter at the beginning of a sentence. You should also use a capital letter for all **proper nouns**.
>
> **Example:** names of people (including the pronoun 'I') and places, days of the week, months of the year, titles and organisations.

E Place one of these verbs into each space so that the sentences make sense. [10]

| escaped | climbed | added | fetched | kicked | knitted |
| melted | played | pounced | ~~pulled~~ | rested | ~~walked~~ |

> **Verbs** are action words that tell us what somebody or something is doing.

Example: *It was cold so she* pulled *on her fleece before she* walked *to school.*

1 Oliver _____ the ball to his sister.
2 Mrs Simpson _____ a scarf for Esther.
3 The tiger _____ on the deer, but the deer _____ .
4 They _____ up the mountain then _____ at the top.
5 We _____ the butter then _____ it to the mixture.
6 They _____ their coats before they _____ outside.

18

Bond SATs Skills Grammar and Punctuation 8–9   **Unit 1**

F) Rewrite the sentences, replacing the underlined words with a pronoun. [5]

Example: *Dan was tired so Dan went to sleep.*

Dan was tired so he went to sleep.

1 Sinan and Patek were upset when the teacher shouted at <u>Sinan and Patek</u>.

_____

_____

2 Mr Pardoe picked up his newspaper and read <u>the newspaper</u>.

_____

_____

3 Dean and Cort played football when <u>Dean and Cort</u> were in the park.

_____

_____

4 Jessie-Mai was happy when <u>Jessie-Mai</u> was chosen to run the race.

_____

_____

5 Sophie and Harry played in the garden with Michael when <u>Michael</u> invited them over.

_____

_____

> A **pronoun** is used in place of a noun. There are different types of **pronoun**.
>
> **Personal pronouns** are used instead of the name of a person, place or object. The **personal pronouns** are: I, me, you, he, him, she, her, it, we, us, they, them.
>
> **Possessive pronouns** tell you who or what owns a noun. The **possessive pronouns** are: my, mine, your, yours, his, her, hers, its, our, ours, their, theirs, whose.

G) Write the singular of these plural words. [4]

Example: *potatoes* potato

1 churches _____   3 mixes _____

2 wives _____   4 calves _____

> A noun is **'singular'** when it refers to one thing and **'plural'** when it refers to more than one thing.

5

9

Unit 1

Bond SATs Skills Grammar and Punctuation 8–9

(H) Write a proper noun from the list below in each space so that the paragraph makes sense. One has been done as an example. [5]

Isle of Wight	January	~~Osborne House~~
Prince Albert	Queen Victoria	Thomas Cubitt

Osborne House is the royal residence where _____

visited each summer with her husband _____.

The builder, _____, built the residence on the

_____ where the sea views are spectacular.

The queen died in the building in the _____

of 1901 when she was 81 years old.

> **Helpful Hint**
> Remember that **proper nouns** are nouns that need a capital letter.
> **Example:** names of people (including 'I') and places, days of the week and months of the year, titles and organisations.

(I) Choose a subordinating conjunction from the list below to join these clauses together. [5]

| although | but | because | ~~so~~ | unless | when |

Example: *It was really hot* **so** *I moved my chair into the shade.*

1 The mouse ran quickly _____ it had just seen the cat.

2 The children were playing in the garden _____ it was now getting dark.

3 "You can't go swimming _____ your brother goes with you."

4 "Please line up in the playground _____ the bell rings."

5 I needed some eggs _____ the shop was shut!

> A **clause** is a **simple sentence** that can be joined to another **clause** by using a **conjunction**. A **conjunction** is a joining word that can be placed at the start or in the middle of a sentence. A **subordinating conjunction** joins a **clause** that is not as important as the main (sometimes called independent) **clause**. The **subordinating conjunctions** include: after, although, as, because, before, it, since, when, while.

Unit 2

Bond SATs Skills Grammar and Punctuation 8–9

A Add a full stop, question mark or exclamation mark to the end of these sentences. [6]

Example: *Our tortoise is called Henry.*

1 Would you mind helping me with these boxes ____

2 Do you know when Sasha is taking her piano exam ____

3 Nikki took all the girls to the birthday party at Rani's house ____

4 There's a fire! Sound the alarm ____

5 Izzy goes to dance club after school on Tuesdays ____

6 Please can you make a cake for Zia's birthday ____

B Rewrite the sentences, making sure there are capital letters and that each one ends with a full stop, question mark or exclamation mark. [6]

Example: *michael and lia both go to st john's infant school*

Michael and Lia both go to St John's Infant School.

1 i caught the train to london this week

2 i love eating strawberry ice cream

3 what is that doing there

4 have you got a key for mr harvey's house

5 shall we make a curry for our supper tonight

6 i have just won first prize

> **Helpful Hint**
>
> Capital letters, **full stops**, **question marks** and **exclamation marks** are really important in your writing. Always check your work in case you have forgotten any of them.

Unit 2

Bond SATs Skills Grammar and Punctuation 8–9

C Copy out these verbs, adding the letters 'ed'. [10]

Example: faint   fainted

1 add   _____
2 box   _____
3 count   _____
4 frighten   _____
5 end   _____
6 fetch   _____
7 gather   _____
8 warm   _____
9 arrest   _____
10 join   _____

> If you can add 'ed' to the end of a **verb**, it is a **regular verb**. Adding 'ed' shows us that the action happened in the past.

D Put a comma after each item in these lists, except before the word 'and'. [4]

Example: My friends are Katie Sam Josh Solomon and Tomas.

My friends are Katie, Sam, Josh, Solomon and Tomas.

1 I bought ham jam mustard custard tomatoes potatoes and bread.
2 My hobbies are reading cycling Brownies and swimming.
3 We will be away on Tuesday Wednesday Thursday Friday and Saturday.
4 The vase was full of roses lilies irises and daisies.

> **Commas** are used in many ways. In a list, a **comma** is used to separate everything except the last item when the word 'and' is used.

E Write the singular of these plural words. [8]

Example: scarves   scarf

1 teeth   _____
2 buses   _____
3 geese   _____
4 men   _____
5 leaves   _____
6 eyes   _____
7 coaches   _____
8 tissues   _____

> 💡 **Helpful Hint**
> Remember that a noun is **singular** when it refers to one thing and **plural** when it refers to more than one thing.

8

22

Unit 2

Bond SATs Skills Grammar and Punctuation 8–9

F Rewrite the sentences, replacing the underlined words with a pronoun. [5]

Example: *Reuben found <u>Reuben's</u> book under the sofa.*

Reuben found his book under the sofa.

1 Grandma took the children on holiday with <u>Grandma</u>.

2 Kieran was playing with Aidan and followed <u>Aidan</u> into the garden.

3 Rajesh caught the ball and then threw <u>the ball</u> to Huawei.

4 The teachers were in the staffroom when the fire alarm disturbed <u>the teachers.</u>

5 Jay found reading difficult but <u>Jay</u> practised hard and got much better at it.

> **Helpful Hint**
>
> Remember that a **pronoun** is used in place of a noun.
>
> **Personal pronouns** are used instead of the name of a person, place, or object.
>
> **Example:** I, me, you, he, him, she, her, it, we, us, they, them
>
> **Possessive pronouns** show who or what owns a noun.
>
> **Example:** my, mine, your, yours, his, her, hers, its, our, ours, their, theirs, whose

Unit 2
Bond SATs Skills Grammar and Punctuation 8–9

G Write a proper noun from the list below in each space so that the paragraph makes sense. One has been done as an example. [5]

> Louisa   March   November
> Shropshire   Thomas Acton   ~~Victorian Farm~~

The television series *Victorian Farm* showed how rural life might have been in 1885.

My great, great grandmother, _____, was born in the county of

_____ at Acton Scott, which was the farm used in the series.

The landowner, _____, chose to keep his farm as it was in the

19th century. Nowadays you can visit the farm as it is open most of the year, from

_____ to _____.

H Label each sentence as a command, a question, a statement or an exclamation. [4]

Example: *When do you go on holiday?*   question

1 Who wants an apple?   _____

2 Do you want to join in our game?   _____

3 Go away!   _____

4 Let's watch a film.   _____

I Turn each question into a command. [4]

Example: *Will you put on your coat?*   *Put on your coat!*

1 Would you like to sit down?   _____

2 Could you please be quiet?   _____

3 Can you stop talking, please?   _____

4 Would you like to open your books?   _____

💡 Helpful Hint

Remember to put the **verb** at the beginning of the sentence to make a **command**. **Commands** sometimes end with an **exclamation mark** (!).

Bond SATs Skills Grammar and Punctuation 8–9

Unit 3

A Add a full stop, question mark or exclamation mark to the end of these sentences. [8]

Example: *Shall we meet at your house?*

1 Are you feeling very hungry____
2 Where is my calculator____
3 Toby said that he was really fed up____
4 Follow that car____
5 I will take my raincoat tomorrow____
6 What time is your hospital appointment____
7 Eva sings in the choir with Fran____
8 Oh no____

> **Helpful Hint**
> Remember that you can use an **exclamation mark** to show that your writing is a **command** or that it is shocking, funny or angry. Use a **question mark** when you ask a **question**. Use a **full stop** at the end of all other sentences.

B Put a comma after each item in these lists, except before the word 'and'. [7]

Example: *We visited Sidmouth Exmouth Topsham and Exeter on our holidays.*

We visited Sidmouth, Exmouth, Topsham and Exeter on our holidays.

1 I am sitting with Maurice Doris Horace Wallace and Sid.
2 The colours of the rainbow are red orange yellow green blue indigo and violet.
3 I love eating beans peas rice dhal and chapattis.
4 The planets are Mercury Venus Earth Mars Jupiter Saturn Uranus and Neptune.
5 We have goats pigs sheep cows chickens ducks and geese.
6 Mermaids unicorns dragons and trolls are all mythical creatures.
7 Swimming tennis football and hockey are Elena's favourite sports.

> **Helpful Hint**
> Remember that a **comma** is used to separate items in a list.

15

Unit 3

Bond SATs Skills Grammar and Punctuation 8–9

Ⓒ Underline the common nouns in these sentences. [6]

Example: *Elsa stuck the <u>postcard</u> on the <u>board</u> with a <u>pin</u>.*

1 Basheer rode his bicycle to the postbox at the end of the road.

2 Mrs Maloney fed the fish and took the dog to the kennels.

3 Soup is popular for lunch at our local cafe.

4 We put the saucepans on the hob as we prepared the carrots.

5 Taking a book from the shelf, Leroy sat on a chair to read.

6 Mr Patel accidentally left his coat and camera on the train.

> A **common noun** is the general name of a person, place or thing.
>
> **Example:** girl, book, supermarket, apple.

Ⓓ Underline the abstract nouns in these sentences. [6]

Example: *Her eyes shone with <u>happiness</u>.*

1 My grandma has a long memory.

2 Have you had any thoughts?

3 My big sister is in love with her boyfriend.

4 Mrs Clee had a wonderful skill in flower arranging.

5 Jack and Joy found strength in their family.

6 His eyes flashed with anger.

> **Abstract nouns** often refer to ideas or feelings. **Abstract nouns** cannot be touched, seen or heard.
>
> **Example:** fear, beauty, health.

Ⓔ Underline 'has' or 'have' so that each sentence makes sense. [6]

Example: *Our house (<u>has</u>/have) a red door.*

1 "That piece of paper (has/have) writing on it."

2 "These beautiful flowers (has/have) just been delivered!"

3 Our grandparents (has/have) bought a caravan.

4 The cows (has/have) spent the day in the field.

5 My dog (has/have) a new ball to play with.

6 "Try the cakes that (has/have) pink icing on them!"

> Use the word 'has' when you talk about one person or thing. Use the word 'have' when you talk about more than one person or thing.
>
> **Example:** She has the books. They have the books.

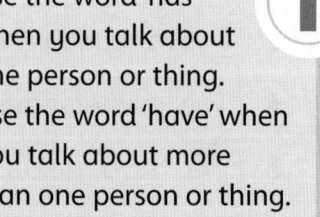

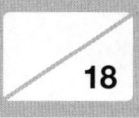

Unit 3

Bond SATs Skills Grammar and Punctuation 8–9

F Add adverbs to these sentences by adding 'ly' to the adjectives in capitals. [5]

> An **adjective** is a word that describes a noun. An **adverb** is a word that describes a **verb**. To make an **adverb** from an **adjective**, add the letters 'ly' to the **adjective**.

Example: *(EXCITED) The two boys yelled* excitedly.

1 (WEAK) The kitten mewed _____.

2 (EXACT) She cut the cake _____.

3 (NEAR) We _____ hit the target.

4 (NEAT) He folded his clothes _____.

5 (CLEAR) He spoke _____ on the telephone.

G Copy out these verbs, adding the letters 'ed'. [6]

Example: *wonder* wondered

1 look _____   4 offer _____

2 melt _____   5 plant _____

3 need _____   6 question _____

> 💡 **Helpful Hint**
> Remember adding 'ed' to a **regular verb** shows the action is in the past.

H Choose a subordinating conjunction from the list below to join these clauses together. [5]

| although | because | until | since | ~~unless~~ | when |

Example: *I can't get to Alex's* unless *Dad takes me.*

1 _____ Aslan tried hard, he still did not win.

2 I have been going to the same dentist _____ I was a child.

3 Our field trip was cancelled at the last minute _____ of heavy rain.

4 You can't go out _____ you polish your shoes!

5 Mum put the suitcases in the car _____ Dad came home.

> 💡 **Helpful Hint**
> Remember that a **subordinating conjunction** is used to join two **clauses** together.

16

Unit 3

Bond SATs Skills Grammar and Punctuation 8–9

Quick quiz

1 Underline the proper noun. donkey   running   Salford
2 Underline the common noun. goat   happiness   Africa
3 Underline the abstract noun. horse   pride   Hampshire
4 Underline the pronoun. there   her   wear
5 Underline the conjunction. him   what   before
6 What are proper nouns? _____

_____

7 What letters can be added to a regular verb to show that the action happened in the past? _____

8 How can you make an adverb from an adjective? _____

_____

9 What are inverted commas for? _____

_____

10 What do 'singular' and 'plural' mean? _____

_____

11 When should you use 'has' and when should you use 'have'? _____

_____

12 What is a verb? _____

_____

13–35 Copy out this paragraph, adding capital letters and punctuation.

alex and ola made a list of the days of the week which is your favourite day alex asked ola well ola replied i like sunday best as i can wake up whenever i want

_____

_____

_____

35

Bond SATs Skills Grammar and Punctuation 8–9

Unit 4

A Rewrite the sentences, making sure there are capital letters and that each one ends with a full stop, question mark or exclamation mark. [6]

Example: *can we go to archie's on saturday*

Can we go to Archie's on Saturday?

1 please come in and sit down, vikram

2 we constructed some models on thursday morning

3 mr hughes sings in the church choir on sundays

4 did luke and erica go to the cinema on saturday

5 stop that at once

6 where are brooke and zara hiding

B Put inverted commas around the words spoken in these sentences. [8]

Example: *Have you got your swimming costume? asked the teacher.*

"Have you got your swimming costume?" asked the teacher.

1 The man called out for his dog, Davie, where are you? Davie, come here!
2 Are you coming fishing? Dad shouted. I'm leaving in five minutes.
3 The Tudors built this house, the teacher said, pointing to the building.
4 The girls shouted to each other, He is there! Look, he is there!
5 Should I turn left at the traffic lights? asked the bus driver.
6 Don't forget to switch off the television before you go.
7 Come on! Keep up! cried Mrs Morgan.
8 We will be leaving in five minutes.

14

Unit 4

Bond SATs Skills Grammar and Punctuation 8–9

C Copy out these verbs, adding the letters 'ed'. [6]

Example: mark marked

1 reach _____
2 sack _____
3 talk _____
4 visit _____
5 work _____
6 yell _____

> **Helpful Hint**
>
> Remember that when you add 'ed' to the end of a **verb**, it shows us that the action is in the past.

D Underline the proper nouns in these sentences. [4]

Example: <u>Josh</u> and <u>I</u> got lost in the maze at <u>Hampton Court Palace</u>.

1 I am reading Oliver Twist by the author Charles Dickens.
2 Jordan won his tennis match at Wimbledon on Friday.
3 Dad will be working in France until August.
4 I will be visiting Blenheim Palace in Oxfordshire.

E Write the past tense of the main verb in the spaces so that the sentences make sense. [4]

> bought   ~~woke~~   taught   went   spoke

Example: I woke up early but I didn't wake my sister until later.

1 Jasmine wants to buy shoes to go with the dress she _____ yesterday.

2 I _____ to Dad about my homework and he will speak to Mum about it.

3 Grandma was _____ how to cook, but today they teach us about healthy eating.

4 This year we will go to Spain by coach but last year we _____ by plane.

> Usually to change a **verb** to past tense, you can add 'ed' (kick + ed = kicked).
>
> **Irregular verbs** do not follow this pattern.
>
> **Example:**
> bite   bit
> break   broke

14

Bond SATs Skills Grammar and Punctuation 8–9   **Unit 4**

F Add 'er' to the end of each verb to make a noun. [8]

> Adding the letters 'er' to the end of some **verbs** will make a noun.

Example: *paint + er = painter*

1 speak + er = _____

2 fight + er = _____

3 walk + er = _____

4 play + er = _____

5 jump + er = _____

6 garden + er = _____

7 toast + er = _____

8 train + er = _____

G Underline 'has' or 'have' so that each sentence makes sense. [12]

Example: *Isobel (has/have) just moved house.*

1 Thomas (has/have) a baby sister.
2 Three of my friends (has/have) joined my dance class.
3 Our parish church (has/have) a steeple.
4 The football team (has/have) scored a goal.
5 Merry and Andrew (has/have) gone on holiday.
6 The walkers (has/have) gone up the mountain.
7 The cat (has/have) been sleeping on the blanket.
8 The birds (has/have) flown south for the winter.
9 (Has/Have) the post been delivered yet?
10 The kettle (has/have) stopped working.
11 We (has/have) lit the lamps to celebrate Diwali.
12 (Has/Have) the books arrived?

 Helpful Hint

Remember to use 'has' when you talk about one person or thing and 'have' when you talk about more than one person or thing.

20

Unit 4
Bond SATs Skills Grammar and Punctuation 8–9

H Put an apostrophe before the 's' to show possession. [4]

Example: *The cat has a collar.* The cat's collar.

1. The man has a beard. _____

2. Mum has a necklace. _____

3. Marion has a goldfish. _____

4. Roshanna has a brother. _____

> Use an apostrophe to show when something belongs to someone. This is called **'possession'**.
>
> **Example:** the bicycle belongs to Graham – Graham's bicycle. The apostrophe usually goes before the 's'.

I Turn these questions into commands. [6]

Example: *Would you please enter the code?* Enter the code.

1. Would you please stop that noise?

   _____

2. Will you line up?

   _____

3. Will you lock the door?

   _____

4. Can you please put your coats on your pegs?

   _____

5. Will you write this down?

   _____

6. Can you please walk in pairs?

   _____

> 💡 **Helpful Hint**
>
> Remember to put the **verb** at the beginning of a sentence to make a **command**. **Commands** sometimes end with an **exclamation mark**.

Unit 5

Bond SATs Skills Grammar and Punctuation 8–9

A Write a proper noun from the list below in each space so that the paragraph makes sense. One has been done as an example. [5]

> Pompeii   Roman   August
> Italy   Mount Vesuvius   ~~Europe~~

The only active volcano in mainland *Europe* is _____ on the west coast of _____. In the month of _____ in the year 79 AD, it erupted violently and destroyed the _____ cities of _____ and Herculaneum.

Helpful Hint
Remember to give **proper nouns** a capital letter.

B Rewrite the sentences, making sure there are capital letters and that each one ends with a full stop, question mark or exclamation mark. [5]

Example: *"that's gorgeous" screamed liu excitedly*

"That's gorgeous!" screamed Liu excitedly.

1 i can't believe you have eaten all of that cake

_____

2 on tuesday i am taking the train from york to cambridge

_____

3 over the summer, tom will be staying with his cousins in weymouth.

_____

4 i booked the last flight to jamaica before easter

_____

5 when are the visiting hours at st mary's hospital

_____

10

Unit 5 Bond SATs Skills Grammar and Punctuation 8–9

C Use an apostrophe to make these words into contractions. [4]

Example: she has *she's*

1 do not _____

2 we are _____

3 I would _____

4 they are _____

> An apostrophe is used to show where letters have been missed out in a word or words. This is called **contraction**.
>
> **Example:** 'I am' becomes 'I'm' and 'you are' becomes 'you're'.

D Fill the gap with a collective noun from the list below. [6]

| bunch | team | choir | ~~group~~ | shoal | library | flock |

Example: *A group of people.*

1 A _____ of singers.

2 A _____ of books.

3 A _____ of fish.

4 A _____ of sheep.

5 A _____ of flowers.

6 A _____ of footballers.

> **Collective nouns** refer to groups of people or things. They are usually counted as **singular** rather than **plural**.
>
> **Example:** A herd of cows.
>
> This is one group of cows.

E Underline the adverbs in these sentences. [8]

Example: *James ate his supper <u>greedily</u>.*

1 I had to think carefully.

2 The teacher shouted angrily at the boys.

3 Dad proudly presented the birthday cake he had made.

4 Daxa slid down the slide gleefully.

5 We closed the door quietly behind us.

6 Unfortunately, I missed the last bus into town.

7 The baby gurgled happily in its pram.

8 Ivan pedalled furiously on his bicycle.

> **Adverbs** are words that describe how an action is done. They usually end in 'ly'.

18

20

Bond SATs Skills Grammar and Punctuation 8–9 **Unit 5**

F Write the singular of these plural words. [8]

Example: women   *Woman*

1 elves   _____

2 feet   _____

3 knives   _____

4 boxes   _____

5 glasses   _____

6 lives   _____

7 fleeces   _____

8 patios   _____

> **Helpful Hint**
>
> Remember that nouns are **singular** when they refer to one thing and **plural** when they refer to more than one thing.

G Rewrite the sentences, replacing the underlined words with a pronoun. [5]

Example: *Sophy was looking forward to Sophy's party.*

  Sophy was looking forward to her party.

1 Juliet took the suitcase with Juliet.

  _____

2 The book is open because I am reading the book.

  _____

3 Mohammad was hungry so Mohammad ate an apple.

  _____

4 The twins often played with Isla and Eve as Isla and Eve lived next door.

  _____

5 Charlotte is baking so Charlotte weighs the flour carefully.

  _____

13

Unit 5

Bond SATs Skills Grammar and Punctuation 8–9

(H) Turn these into simple sentences by crossing out all of the unnecessary words. Just keep the five words needed for each sentence to make sense. [8]

> A **simple sentence** has a **verb** and a **noun** but it does not have a **conjunction**.
>
> **Example:** Our cousin has a new, red car.

Example: The first train for Bristol was running really late.

The first train ~~for Bristol~~ was ~~running really~~ late.

1 I went for a lovely walk by the river.
2 Our new cat simply loves her soft bed!
3 As a treat, we went to the cinema to see the latest film.
4 The apple trees in the orchard looked lovely covered in blossom.
5 She is wearing a long woollen cardigan.
6 The bank near the bridge is closed tomorrow.
7 Those bees swarmed from their hive last week.
8 The huge, greedy dog ate the hot, delicious sausages.

(I) Add 'er' to the end of each verb to make a noun. [10]

Example: think + er = thinker

1 build + er = _____
2 teach + er = _____
3 read + er = _____
4 dress + er = _____
5 sweep + er = _____
6 pack + er = _____
7 mow + er = _____
8 keep + er = _____
9 cook + er = _____
10 heat + er = _____

18

Answers

Bond SATs Skills Grammar and Punctuation 8–9

Unit 1

A 1 question 2 statement 3 command 4 exclamation 5 question 6 command 7 statement 8 exclamation 9 question 10 exclamation 11 statement 12 command

B 1 ./! 2 . 3 ? 4 ./! 5 ? 6 !

C 1 "Sit, you naughty dog," the woman said. "Sit!"
2 The man asked the guard, "What time is the next train to Bristol?"
3 "Would you like to come to our party?" the twins asked.
4 "I can't see you anywhere," Pip said. "Where are you?"

D 1 Mrs Jones, Ashford Primary School, Thursday
2 Gareth, Mrs McCurdy, Owen
3 Ivanka, Lincoln, October
4 Poppy, Tuesday

E 1 kicked 2 knitted 3 pounced, escaped 4 climbed, rested 5 melted, added 6 fetched, played

F 1 them 2 it 3 they 4 she 5 he

G 1 church 2 wife 3 mix 4 calf

H 1 Queen Victoria 2 Prince Albert 3 Thomas Cubitt 4 Isle of Wight 5 January

I 1 because 2 although 3 unless 4 when 5 but

Unit 2

A 1 ? 2 ? 3 . 4 ! 5 . 6 ?

B 1 I caught the train to London this week.
2 I love eating strawberry ice cream./!
3 What is that doing there?
4 Have you got a key for Mr Harvey's house?
5 Shall we make a curry for our supper tonight?
6 I have just won first prize./!

C 1 added 2 boxed 3 counted 4 frightened 5 ended 6 fetched 7 gathered 8 warmed 9 arrested 10 joined

D 1 I bought ham, jam, mustard, custard, tomatoes, potatoes and bread.
2 My hobbies are reading, cycling, Brownies and swimming.
3 We will be away on Tuesday, Wednesday, Thursday, Friday and Saturday.
4 The vase was full of roses, lilies, irises and daisies

E 1 tooth 2 bus 3 goose 4 man 5 leaf 6 eye 7 coach 8 tissue

F 1 her 2 him 3 it 4 them 5 he

G 1 Louisa 2 Shropshire 3 Thomas Acton 4 March 5 November

H 1 question 2 question 3 command 4 statement

I 1 Sit down./! 2 Be quiet./! 3 Stop talking./! 4 Open your books./!

Unit 3

A 1 ? 2 ? 3 ./! 4 ! 5 . 6 ? 7 . 8 !

B 1 I am sitting with Maurice, Doris, Horace, Wallace and Sid.
2 The colours of the rainbow are red, orange, yellow, green, blue, indigo and violet.
3 I love eating beans, peas, rice, dhal and chapattis.
4 The planets are Mercury, Venus, Earth, Mars, Jupiter, Saturn, Uranus and Neptune.
5 We have goats, pigs, sheep, cows, chickens, ducks and geese.
6 Mermaids, unicorns, dragons and trolls are all mythical creatures.
7 Swimming, tennis, football and hockey are Elena's favourite sports.

C 1 bicycle, postbox, road 2 fish, dog, kennels 3 soup, lunch, cafe 4 saucepans, hob, carrots 5 book, shelf, chair 6 coat, camera, train

D 1 memory 2 thoughts 3 love 4 skill 5 strength 6 anger

E 1 has 2 have 3 have 4 have 5 has 6 have

F 1 weakly 2 exactly 3 nearly 4 neatly 5 clearly

G 1 looked 2 melted 3 needed 4 offered 5 planted 6 questioned

H 1 Although 2 since 3 because 4 until 5 when

Bond SATs Skills Grammar and Punctuation 8–9

Quick quiz
1 Salford 2 goat 3 pride 4 her 5 before
6 Proper nouns have a capital letter and include names of people (including 'I') and places, days of the week and months of the year, titles and organisations.
7 'ed'
8 You can add 'ly' to an adjective to make an adverb.
9 Inverted commas are used to surround dialogue/words spoken.
10 Singular means one, plural means more than one.
11 The word 'has' should be used with the singular and the word 'have' should be used with the plural.
12 A verb is an action/doing word.

13–35 **A**lex and **O**la made a list of the days of the week. "**W**hich is your favourite day**?**" **A**lex asked **O**la.
"**W**ell**,**" **O**la replied**,** "**I** like **S**unday best as **I** can wake up whenever **I** want**!**"
(Final exclamation mark could be a full stop.)

Unit 4

(A) 1 Please come in and sit down, Vikram.
2 We constructed some models on Thursday morning.
3 Mr Hughes sings in the church choir on Sundays.
4 Did Luke and Erica go to the cinema on Saturday?
5 Stop that at once./!
6 Where are Brooke and Zara hiding?

(B) 1 The man called out for his dog, "Davie, where are you? Davie, come here!"
2 "Are you coming fishing?" Dad shouted. "I'm leaving in five minutes."
3 "The Tudors built this house," the teacher said, pointing to the building.
4 The girls shouted to each other, "He is there! Look, he is there!"
5 "Should I turn left at the traffic lights?" asked the bus driver.
6 "Don't forget to switch off the television before you go."
7 "Come on! Keep up!" cried Mrs Morgan.
8 "We will be leaving in five minutes."

(C) 1 reached 3 talked 5 worked
2 sacked 4 visited 6 yelled

(D) 1 *Oliver Twist*, Charles Dickens
2 Jordan, Wimbledon, Friday
3 Dad, France, August
4 Blenheim Palace, Oxfordshire

(E) 1 bought 2 spoke 3 taught 4 went

(F) 1 speaker 4 player 7 toaster
2 fighter 5 jumper 8 trainer
3 walker 6 gardener

(G) 1 has 4 has 7 has 10 has
2 have 5 have 8 have 11 have
3 has 6 have 9 has 12 have

(H) 1 The man's beard. 3 Marion's goldfish.
2 Mum's necklace. 4 Roshanna's brother.

(I) 1 Stop that noise./! 4 Put your coats on your pegs./!
2 Line up./! 5 Write this down./!
3 Lock the door./! 6 Walk in pairs./!

Unit 5

(A) 1 Mount Vesuvius 3 August 5 Pompeii
2 Italy 4 Roman

(B) 1 I can't believe you have eaten all of that cake!
2 On Tuesday I am taking the train from York to Cambridge.
3 Over the summer, Tom will be staying with his cousins in Weymouth.
4 I booked the last flight to Jamaica before Easter./!
5 When are the visiting hours at St Mary's Hospital?

(C) 1 don't 2 we're 3 I'd 4 they're

(D) 1 choir 3 shoal 5 bunch
2 library 4 flock 6 team

(E) 1 carefully 4 gleefully 7 happily
2 angrily 5 quietly 8 furiously
3 proudly 6 Unfortunately

(F) 1 elf 3 knife 5 glass 7 fleece
2 foot 4 box 6 life 8 patio

(G) 1 her 2 it 3 he 4 they 5 she

(H) 1 I went for a walk.
2 Our cat loves her bed!
3 We went to the cinema.
4 The apple trees looked lovely.
5 She is wearing a cardigan.
6 The bank is closed tomorrow.
7 Bees swarmed from their hive.
8 The dog ate the sausages.

(I) 1 builder 4 dresser 7 mower 10 heater
2 teacher 5 sweeper 8 keeper
3 reader 6 packer 9 cooker

Unit 6

(A) 1 ? 2 . 3 ./! 4 ./! 5 ? 6 ?

(B) 1 because 2 but 3 unless 4 as 5 When

Bond SATs Skills Grammar and Punctuation 8–9

C 1 "How many times did I ask you?" Mum said crossly.
   2 The man knocked on the door. "Hello! Is anybody in?"
   3 "Are we nearly there?" the children asked. "When will we see the sea?"
   4 I picked up the phone. "Hello, can you hear me?" I said.
   5 "Our tortoise hibernates over the winter," Mrs Hughes explained.
   6 "Have you ever watched a horse race?" asked the jockey.
   7 "Well!" exclaimed Ash. "It's been ages since I last saw you!"
   8 "Remember to wear reflective clothing when you are cycling," the teacher said.

D 1 The dog's ball.   3 Matthew's pencil.
   2 Hashmee's book.   4 Zara's doll.

E 1 imagination   2 faith   3 idea   4 judgement

F 1 pretty, flowery   3 cheeky, ripe
   2 fresh, hot

G 1 lorries   3 jellies   5 countries
   2 bodies   4 memories   6 skies

H 1 has   3 has   5 has
   2 has   4 have   6 have

I 1 warmly   3 yearly   5 quietly
   2 stupidly 4 foolishly

Quick quiz

1 swarm
2 while
3 slowly
4 "How did you get in?" I asked my dog.
5 rent
6 curious
7 drove
8 sing
9 Chloe's ball.
10 Fetch the key!/Fetch the key.
11–12 berries, flies
13 He, them
14 The rabbit ate the carrot.
15 fiercely
16–19 you're, we're, I'd, they're

Unit 7

A 1 ?   2 !   3 ?   4 ./!   5 !   6 .

B 1 she's   3 couldn't   5 they'd
   2 they'll   4 I'll   6 they're

C 1 table, chairs, kitchen   4 donkey, stable, hay
   2 gloves, hat, weather   5 teacher, school, months
   3 television, game, book   6 boats, harbour, day

D 1 range   2 orchestra   3 pack   4 pride

E 1 a   2 c   3 a

F 1 singer   3 worker   5 boiler   7 hanger
   2 boxer   4 seller   6 chatterer 8 talker

G 1 drink   4 pinch   7 were   10 went
   2 eat   5 saw   8 am
   3 mows   6 stopped 9 known

H 1 tightly   3 brightly   5 fondly
   2 suddenly   4 sharply   6 honestly

I 1 but   2 and   3 but   4 and   5 or

J (Some variation with wording in the following four sentences is acceptable as long as the actual speech isn't directly quoted.)
   1 Mum asked Alfie to tidy his room.
   2 Lijuan asked her mum if she could make some cakes.
   3 Mr Chakrabarti said that we were all welcome in his home.
   4 Our neighbour explained that Mrs Onslow had a new grandson.
   5 Seb called out to his friend to come over.

Unit 8

A 1–3 "Class 2, Sit down!" said Mrs Baggott as she looked around. "Are we all here?"
   "No, Mrs Baggott," said a little girl. "Mahari is missing."
   "Where is she?" Mrs Baggott asked.
   4–6 "There is a dragon in the village!" Paul cried.
   "A dragon?" his mother responded. "Are you sure it is a dragon?"
   "Well, it was creature breathing fire," Paul replied breathlessly.

B 1 Come with me./!   3 Eat your vegetables./!
   2 Play that song again./! 4 Change the batteries./!

C 1 ✗   2 ✗   3 ✓   4 ✓   5 ✗

D 1 you'd   2 wouldn't   3 we'll   4 can't

E 1 The woman's basket.   3 The traveller's caravan.
   2 The dog's lead.   4 The snake's skin.

F 1 smartly   5 nervously   9 confidently
   2 quietly   6 punctually   10 brightly
   3 noisily   7 regularly
   4 skilfully 8 continuously

G 1–5 **M**y, **M**ay, **D**evon, **I**, *Chocolate*

H 1 have   3 has   5 have   7 have
   2 have   4 have   6 Has   8 has

A3

I 1	Mars	2	Olympus Mons	3	Mount Everest	
J 1	strangely	3	monthly	5	constantly	
2	softly	4	hopefully	6	wisely	

Unit 9

A 1 when 2 since 3 Unless 4 Because 5 Although

B 1 he   3 him   5 it   7 her
   2 she   4 They   6 their

C 1 We break up on Friday for the summer holidays.
   2 How far is it from Inverness to Oban?
   3 Ibrahim turned around slowly with great excitement.
   4 Go and fetch Mr Nash from the office./!

D 1 The forest's trees.
   2 The swimming pool's slide.
   3 The bag's handle.
   4 Our car's sunroof.

E 1 hammer, screwdriver, toolbox
   2 cups, plates, dishwasher
   3 monkeys, lions, elephants, penguins, zoo
   4 chapattis, dosas, bhajis, paneer, picnic
   5 visitors, cathedral, river
   6 photographs, building, camera

F 1 a   2 b   3 a

G 1 hold   3 plays   5 are   7 know
   2 paints 4 reads   6 is   8 have

H 1 loosely   3 gratefully   5 effortlessly
   2 loudly   4 proudly   6 beautifully

I *(Some variation with wording in the following four sentences is acceptable as long as the actual speech isn't directly quoted.)*
   1 Niamh asked her father if he could make a tree house.
   2 The teacher warned the class that the fire alarm would ring in ten minutes.
   3 Flora said that she would like an apple.
   4 Bertie told his sister to turn the computer off straight away.

Unit 10

1 bunch, flight   3 dream, hope
2 fleet, shoal   4 talent, skill

5 old, red, bumpy   6 warm, brightly, sparkling
7 with the red front door
8 with its many narrow alleys
9 The chef told the cooks that they needed to beat the eggs well.
10 Although
11–12 "My name is Vijay," the little boy said, looking around at the other boys in the hall.
"Welcome!" said the kind-looking leader. "I am sure that you will enjoy Cubs."
13 Joe is upstairs in his bedroom.
14 I will put the kettle on for a cup of tea.
15 has   17 He, them   19 sings
16 have   18 They, they   20 performing
21 carefully, quickly
22 steadily, successfully
23 sprinter
24 climber
25 slyly
26 jointly
27 briskly
28 clearly
29–45 "**W**e are going to the seaside!" said **D**ad.
"I've packed a picnic and got your swimming costumes!" called **M**um**,** as we ran upstairs to find our buckets**,** spades**,** inflatable dolphin and the beach balls.
Dad laughed and went to load the car**.**
(First two exclamation marks could be full stops.)
46 Turn off the light./!
47 Clean your teeth./!
48 Tell me where you put the keys?
49 Pay attention./!
50 conjunction
51 question mark
52 inverted commas
53 commas
54 apostrophe
55 's'
56 adjective
57 adverb
58 pronoun
59 adjectival
60 regular

Unit 6

Bond SATs Skills Grammar and Punctuation 8–9

A Add a full stop, question mark or exclamation mark to the end of these sentences. [6]

Example: *Ruby is coming home on Thursday.*

1 Can you see the fish in the pond ____
2 The wind blew the leaves off the trees ____
3 Don't stand on the chair ____
4 Turn the television off ____
5 Where are the library books ____
6 How much milk do we have in the fridge ____

B Choose a subordinating conjunction from the list below to join these clauses together. [5]

| ~~although~~ | because | unless | but | as | when |

Example: *Although I ran quickly, I didn't win the race.*

1 The woman was getting cross _____ the dogs would not stop barking.
2 The children put their coats on _____ it was too soon to go home.
3 We can't go to the cinema _____ Mum takes us into town.
4 James could not visit yesterday _____ he had a music exam.
5 _____ we visited the farm last week, we saw some piglets.

C Put inverted commas around the words spoken in these sentences. [8]

Example: *That's wonderful news! said Florence. You will have a great time.*

"*That's wonderful news!*" *said Florence.* "*You will have a great time.*"

1 How many times did I ask you? Mum said crossly.
2 The man knocked on the door. Hello! Is anybody in?
3 Are we nearly there? the children asked. When will we see the sea?
4 I picked up the phone. Hello, can you hear me? I said.
5 Our tortoise hibernates over the winter, Mrs Hughes explained.
6 Have you ever watched a horse race? asked the jockey.
7 Well! exclaimed Ash. It's been ages since I last saw you!
8 Remember to wear reflective clothing when you are cycling, the teacher said.

19

Unit 6

Bond SATs Skills Grammar and Punctuation 8–9

D Put an apostrophe before the 's' to show possession. [4]

Example: *The girl has a temper.* The girl's temper.

1 The dog has a ball. _____

2 Hashmee has a book. _____

3 Matthew has a pencil. _____

4 Zara has a doll. _____

E Underline the abstract nouns in these sentences. [4]

Example: *He was praised for his <u>bravery</u>.*

1 Stacey has a good imagination.

2 I have faith that we will win the football match.

3 Dad had a brilliant idea to build a tree house.

4 The referee used his judgement to allow the game to carry on.

> 💡 **Helpful Hint**
>
> Remember that **abstract nouns** often refer to ideas or feelings. **Abstract nouns** cannot be touched, seen or heard.
>
> **Example:** dream, honesty.

F Put an adjective from the list below before each noun in these sentences. [6]

| cheeky | pretty | hot | fresh |
| ~~ancient~~ | ~~tall~~ | flowery | ripe |

Example: *The ancient forest has lots of tall trees growing in it.*

1 She wore a _____ dress with a _____ pattern to the party.

2 The smell of _____ bread and _____ chocolate was delicious.

3 The _____ monkey stole a _____ banana!

> 💡 **Helpful Hint**
>
> Remember that an **adjective** is a word that describes a noun.

14

Unit 6

Bond SATs Skills Grammar and Punctuation 8–9

G Write the plural word of these singular words by changing the 'y' to an 'i', then adding 'es'. [6]

Example: *baby* babies

1 lorry _____
2 body _____
3 jelly _____
4 memory _____
5 country _____
6 sky _____

H Underline 'has' or 'have' so that each sentence makes sense. [6]

Example: *We (has/have) tickets to see the show.*

1 The shoal of fish (has/have) been moved to the new tank.
2 My baby sister (has/have) a pink teddy bear.
3 The school choir (has/have) been invited to perform in a concert.
4 Those sweets (has/have) been in that bag for weeks!
5 Nobody in the group (has/have) visited this castle before.
6 The horses (has/have) a race to run!

> **Helpful Hint**
>
> Remember to use the word 'has' when you talk about one person or thing. Use the word 'have' when you talk about more than one person or thing. A **collective noun** is usually counted as a single thing.

I Add adverbs to these sentences by adding 'ly' to the adjectives in capitals. [5]

Example: *(LOUD) The alarm rang* loudly.

1 (WARM) The family greeted their guests _____.
2 (STUPID) Max _____ ran across the road without looking first.
3 (YEAR) We had our _____ appointment.
4 (FOOLISH) The boy _____ approached the flames.
5 (QUIET) The children were whispering _____.

17

Unit 6

Bond SATs Skills Grammar and Punctuation 8–9

Quick quiz

1 Underline the collective noun.   singer   envy   swarm

2 Underline the subordinating conjunction.   finding   while   them

3 Underline the adverb.   handbag   red   slowly

4 Add inverted commas to this sentence.

   How did you get in? I asked my dog.

5 Underline the regular verb that the letters 'ed' can be added to.   rent   run   ride

6 Choose an adjective to put before the noun so that the sentence makes sense.

   The _____ llamas approached the girl at the gate.   extremely   snoring   curious

7 Underline the correct verb so that the sentence makes sense.

   We drove/drive/drived to the doctors.

8 Which verb can we add 'er' to the end of to make a noun?   wake   bread   sing

9 Write this sentence using an apostrophe to show possession.

   Chloe has a ball. _____

10 Make a command from this question.

    Would you like to fetch the key? _____

11–12 Change these singular words to plurals using the correct ending.

    berry _____   fly _____

13 Replace the underlined nouns with pronouns.

    Nick took Liam and Finlay to the park.

    _____

14 Remove the unnecessary words to make a simple sentence of five words.

    The rabbit hopped quickly across the floor and ate the carrot.

    _____

15 Use the adjective in capitals to make an adverb in this sentence.

    (FIERCE) The dog growled _____ at the postman.

16–19 Use an apostrophe to make these words into contractions.

    you are _____   I would _____

    we are _____   they are _____

30   19

Unit 7

Bond SATs Skills Grammar and Punctuation 8–9

A Add a full stop, question mark or exclamation mark to the end of these sentences. [6]

Example: *That's unbelievable!*

1 Why are you feeling sad____
2 Oh no, not again____
3 Whose coats are those____
4 I have learnt all of my spellings____
5 Put that priceless vase down____
6 Lucy is going to learn how to ride a bicycle at the weekend____

B Use an apostrophe to make these words into contractions. [6]

Example: *they have   they've*

1 she is   _____
2 they will   _____
3 could not   _____
4 I will   _____
5 they would   _____
6 they are   _____

Helpful Hint

Remember that an apostrophe must go where the missing letter(s) should be.

C Underline the common nouns in these sentences. [6]

Example: *He put butter and jam on his toast.*

1 There is a table and four chairs in our kitchen.
2 I always wear gloves and a hat when the weather is cold.
3 Shall we watch the television, play a game or read a book?
4 The donkey is in the stable eating hay.
5 My teacher has worked in our school for six months.
6 The boats sailed into the harbour at the end of the day.

Unit 7

Bond SATs Skills Grammar and Punctuation 8–9

D Fill the gap with a collective noun from the list below. [4]

| pack | pride | orchestra | ~~school~~ | range |

Example: A *school* of dolphins.

1   A _____ of mountains.   3   A _____ of dogs.

2   An _____ of musicians.   4   A _____ of lions.

> **Helpful Hint**
> Remember that **collective nouns** are used to describe groups of people or things. They are usually counted as **singular** things rather than **plural**.

E Tick the adjectival phrase that is missing in these sentences. [3]

> An **adjectival phrase** is a group of words that describe a noun.

Example: The hotel _____ had wonderful sea views.

   a   with sea views   ☐
   b   on the coast   ☑
   c   which was cute and cuddly   ☐

1   The rain had made the grass, _____ wet and muddy.

   a   which is usually lovely and green,   ☐
   b   and the sea,   ☐
   c   hard and crunchy,   ☐

2   This book, _____ was a birthday present.

   a   I can read quickly,   ☐
   b   a jigsaw puzzle,   ☐
   c   with its bright gold cover, ☐

3   My grandma, _____ loves to swim in the sea.

   a   who will be 80 next year,   ☐
   b   and I,   ☐
   c   soft and gentle,   ☐

Unit 7

Bond SATs Skills Grammar and Punctuation 8–9

F Add the letters 'er' to the end of each verb to make a noun. [8]

Example: design + er = designer

1 sing + er = _____
2 box + er = _____
3 work + er = _____
4 sell + er = _____
5 boil + er = _____
6 chatter + er = _____
7 hang + er = _____
8 talk + er = _____

G Underline the correct verb so that the sentences make sense. [10]

Example: *The man (take/<u>takes</u>) a seat.*

1 We (drink/drinks) our cups of tea.
2 The cows (eat/eats) the grass.
3 The gardener (mow/mows) the grass.
4 My brothers (pinch/pinches) all of the cakes.
5 I (saw/seen) my friend in town this afternoon.
6 The police officer (stop/stopped) the traffic after the road accident.
7 We (was/were) going into town when the bus broke down.
8 I (am/is) finding the problem difficult to solve.
9 We have (know/known) each other all our lives.
10 We (go/went) to the cinema yesterday.

H Add adverbs to these sentences by adding 'ly' to the adjectives in capitals. [6]

Example: *(GENTLE) The waves lapped gently against the shore.*

1 (TIGHT) The girl fastened her coat up _____.
2 (SUDDEN) The wind _____ whipped the newspaper up into the air.
3 (BRIGHT) The candles shone _____ in the dining room.
4 (SHARP) The teacher spoke _____ to the class.
5 (FOND) The little boy hugged his grandma _____.
6 (HONEST) Tim answered the question as _____ as he could.

24

Unit 7

Bond SATs Skills Grammar and Punctuation 8–9

(I) Choose a coordinating conjunction to join the clauses in these sentences together. [5]

| and | but | or |

Example: *Where are we going **and** when will we get there?*

1 The boy was disappointed to lose _____ he still congratulated the winner.

2 First, Mum went to the shops _____ then she went to see Uncle Peter.

3 It was raining hard _____ my umbrella kept me dry.

4 I watched a film _____ then I went to judo.

5 We could either go on holiday to Turkey _____ we could go back to Greece.

> A **conjunction** joins two **clauses** together. There are different types of **conjunction**. A **coordinating conjunction** joins **clauses** together that are equally important.
>
> **Example:** and, but, or.

(J) Turn the direct speech into indirect speech. [5]

Example: *"We are all going on a trip!" said the teacher.*

The teacher told them that they were going on a trip.

1 "Tidy your room, please!" Mum said to Alfie.

_____

2 "Can I make some cakes?" Lijuan asked her mum.

_____

3 "You are all welcome in our home," Mr Chakrabarti said.

_____

4 "Mrs Onslow has a new grandson!" our neighbour explained.

_____

5 "Come over here," Seb called out to his friend.

_____

> **Inverted commas** are used in **direct speech**. They separate the words someone says from the rest of the sentence.
> **Indirect** (or 'reported') **speech** is used if you are explaining what someone has said.
>
> **Example:**
> **Direct speech:** "How much is that?" Kamal asked the shopkeeper.
>
> **Indirect speech:** Kamal asked the shopkeeper how much it was.

10

Unit 8

Bond SATs Skills Grammar and Punctuation 8–9

A This speech is all mixed up! Copy it out and put each person's speech on a new line so that it makes sense. [6]

> Every time a character begins a new speech, use a new line so that it is clear who is speaking.

Example: *"When is my birthday?" Nikolas asked his mum.*

"It is the month after Christmas," Mum answered. "Which month comes after December?"

"Is it January?" Nikolas suggested.

1–3 "Class 2, Sit down!" said Mrs Baggott as she looked around. "Are we all here?" "No, Mrs Baggott," said a little girl. "Mahari is missing." "Where is she?" Mrs Baggott asked.

_____

_____

_____

_____

_____

_____

4–6 "There is a dragon in the village!" Paul cried. "A dragon?" his mother responded. "Are you sure it is a dragon?" "Well, it was a creature breathing fire," Paul replied breathlessly.

_____

_____

_____

_____

_____

_____

> **Helpful Hint**
> Remember that whenever someone speaks, the words that they say must have **inverted commas** at the beginning and end of the speech. The **inverted commas** must include all of the spoken words as well as the punctuation.

Unit 8   Bond SATs Skills Grammar and Punctuation 8–9

B Turn these questions into commands. [4]

Example: *Will you do as you are told?* Do as you're told!

1 Would you like to come with me?

_____

2 Could you play that song again?

_____

3 Will you eat your vegetables?

_____

4 Could you change the batteries?

_____

C Here are some sentences. Put a tick next to the sentences that are written with correct punctuation and capital letters. Put a cross next to the sentences that are written with mistakes. [5]

Example: *Mr and Mrs Khan are going to the cinema on Wednesday.* ✓

Could the baby come to the party. ✗

1 "Would Connor and Ron like to come to dave's birthday party?" ☐

2 Philip and i visited Kathleen in South Africa last summer. ☐

3 "I don't believe you!" responded Marta angrily. ☐

4 I have knitted a scarf for Beth. ☐

5 "well I never!" exclaimed Mrs Anderson in surprise. ☐

D Use an apostrophe to make these words into contractions. [4]

Example: *I am* I'm

1 you would _____   3 we will _____

2 would not _____   4 can not _____

> 💡 **Helpful Hint**
> Remember that an apostrophe must go where the missing letter(s) should be.

E Put an apostrophe before the 's' to show possession. [4]

Example: *The blackbird has a nest.* The blackbird's nest.

1 The woman has a basket.

2 The dog has a lead.

3 The traveller has a caravan.

4 The snake has skin.

F Underline the adverbs in these sentences. [10]

Example: *We lost the match <u>spectacularly</u>.*

1 The soldiers marched smartly across the yard.
2 Vishni talked quietly to his friend Laurie.
3 We splashed noisily in the swimming pool.
4 Mo batted the cricket ball skilfully.
5 Florence knocked on the door nervously.
6 He always arrives punctually.
7 We regularly walk to school.
8 The phone seemed to ring continuously.
9 The cat jumped confidently onto the windowsill.
10 The candles flickered brightly in the darkness.

G Underline the five letters that should be capital letters in this paragraph. [5]

my uncle lives in London and he visits us every year in may. Now that we live by the sea in devon, i think that he loves coming more than ever! In the first week of August, he is taking us to the theatre to see *Charlie and the chocolate Factory*.

Helpful Hint

Remember that **proper nouns** include names of people, places, days of the week and months of the year, titles and organisations. They always start with a capital letter.

Unit 8　　Bond SATs Skills Grammar and Punctuation 8–9

H Underline 'has' or 'have' so that each sentence makes sense. [8]

Example: *What (has/have) you and Lukas been doing today?*

1 How many times (has/have) the twins played on the bouncy castle?

2 The cherry trees (has/have) blossom on them in the spring.

3 The chair (has/have) a comfortable cushion.

4 We (has/have) not been on holiday yet this summer.

5 Those spoons (has/have) been washed and dried.

6 (Has/Have) the cake finished cooking yet?

7 What (has/have) you been doing today?

8 Lena (has/have) broken her arm.

I Write a proper noun from the list below in each space so that the paragraph makes sense. One has been done as an example. [3]

| Mount Everest   Roman   Olympus Mons   Mars |

Named after the *Roman* god of war, the planet _____

is the fourth planet from our sun. Its mountain _____

is the tallest in the solar system. It is 25 kilometres high – three times higher than

_____ on Earth.

J Add adverbs to these sentences by adding 'ly' to the adjectives in capitals. [6]

Example: *(CONFIDENT) The girl recited the poem* confidently.

1 (STRANGE) The police officer looked at him quite _____.

2 (SOFT) The snow was falling _____ on the ground.

3 (MONTH) The magazine was issued _____.

4 (HOPEFUL) The dog looked _____ at his owner.

5 (CONSTANT) Archie was _____ in trouble with his teacher for talking in class.

6 (WISE) Miss Tang nodded _____ when Louise explained her problem.

17

Bond SATs Skills Grammar and Punctuation 8–9

Unit 9

A Choose a subordinating conjunction from the list below to join these clauses together. [5]

| ~~when~~   although   since   unless   when   because |

Example: *Maria had to go to the dentist **when** she got toothache.*

1 The little lamb ran to the sheep _____ she bleated.

2 We have enjoyed swimming _____ we were very young.

3 _____ we can raise the money, we won't be able to build the new hospital.

4 _____ Year 3 were so noisy during lessons, they had to stay in at break time.

5 _____ we didn't go to the park, we still had a fun time.

B Rewrite the sentences, replacing the underlined words with a pronoun. [7]

Example: *Isaac and Amelie like to play tennis when <u>Isaac and Amelie</u> go to the sports club.*

Isaac and Amelie like to play tennis when they go to the sports club.

1 Zac was going to draw so <u>Zac</u> got his crayons and some paper.

_____

2 Mum was using the computer so <u>Mum</u> sat at the table.

_____

3 Jack took the money with <u>Jack</u>.

_____

4 Fu and Jia were playing with Ti and Han. <u>Fu and Jia</u> often played with friends.

_____

5 Dad hated the rain. He was growing sick of <u>the rain</u>.

_____

6 The team play at <u>the team's</u> home ground every Saturday.

_____

7 Everyone was excited because the panda was going to have <u>the panda's</u> baby very soon.

_____

12

Unit 9

Bond SATs Skills Grammar and Punctuation 8–9

C Rewrite the sentences, making sure there are capital letters and that each one ends with a full stop, question mark or exclamation mark. [4]

Example: *in october, i am going to stay with dad in norwich*

> In October, I am going to stay with Dad in Norwich.

1 we break up on friday for the summer holidays

_____

2 how far is it from inverness to oban

_____

3 ibrahim turned around slowly with great excitement

_____

4 go and fetch mr nash from the office

_____

D Put an apostrophe before the 's' to show possession. [4]

Example: *The radio has a battery.* The radio's battery.

1 The forest has trees. _____

2 The swimming pool has a slide. _____

3 The bag has a handle. _____

4 Our car has a sunroof. _____

E Underline the common nouns in these sentences. [6]

Example: *The <u>telephone</u> rang loudly on the <u>desk</u>.*

1 Mum put her hammer and screwdriver in the toolbox.

2 "Will you put the cups and plates in the dishwasher, please?"

3 I saw the monkeys, lions, elephants and penguins at the zoo.

4 We had chappatis, dosas, bhajis and paneer at the picnic.

5 The visitors wandered slowly around the cathedral beside the river.

6 Orla took photographs of the building with her camera.

Unit 9

Bond SATs Skills Grammar and Punctuation 8–9

F Tick the adjectival phrase that is missing in these sentences. [3]

Example: *The shop _____ sells postcards.*

   a at the centre of the village ☑

   b sells stamps and envelopes ☐

   c that lives near the bus stop ☐

1 The _____ dog slowly wandered down the lane.

   a friendly old ☐

   b quickly running and jumping ☐

   c dog called Keith ☐

2 We stayed on holiday in a _____ caravan.

   a dark, blue, underwater ☐

   b smart, green and cream ☐

   c tall, thin, pointed ☐

3 Mr Suffield has a _____ car.

   a shiny, red and brand-new ☐

   b pretty little kitten ☐

   c soft, grey, wool ☐

> **Helpful Hint**
>
> An **adjectival phrase** is a group of words that describe a noun.

G Underline the correct verb so that the sentences make sense. [8]

Example: *Adam (laugh/laughs) at Milo's joke.*

1. The girls (hold/holds) the skipping rope.
2. The artist (paint/paints) a picture.
3. Lucien (play/plays) with his farm animals.
4. The teacher (read/reads) a book to the class.
5. The trees (is/are) dropping their leaves.
6. Gabriela (is/are) going to visit her family in Poland.
7. We (know/knows) which way to go at the roundabout.
8. What shall we (has/have) for lunch?

Unit 9

Bond SATs Skills Grammar and Punctuation 8–9

(H) Add adverbs to these sentences by adding 'ly' to the adjectives in capitals. [6]

Example: *(BRAVE) Igor bravely tried to stop the thief.*

1 (LOOSE) He fastened his tie _____.

2 (LOUD) The class were talking _____.

3 (GRATEFUL) The birthday girl accepted the present _____.

4 (PROUD) The peacock showed off his beautiful tail _____.

5 (EFFORTLESS) The athlete jumped over the hurdles _____.

6 (BEAUTIFUL) Her wedding dress fitted _____.

(I) Turn the direct speech into indirect speech. [4]

Example: *"What time do we have to leave?" asked Mei.*
    Mei asked what time they had to leave.

1 "Can you make a tree house?" Niamh asked her father.

   _____

   _____

2 "The fire alarm will ring in ten minutes," the teacher warned the class.

   _____

   _____

3 "I'd like an apple please," Flora said.

   _____

   _____

4 "You must turn the computer off now!" Bertie said to his sister.

   _____

   _____

> **Helpful Hint**
>
> Remember that **inverted commas** are used to show speech. They separate the words someone says from the rest of the sentence. Indirect (or 'reported') speech is used if you are explaining what someone has said.

10

Bond SATs Skills Grammar and Punctuation 8–9

Unit 10

Test your skills

1–2 **Underline the collective nouns.**

Isla brought me a bunch of grapes after I fell down the flight of stairs.

The fleet of ships followed the shoal of fish.

3–4 **Underline the abstract nouns.**

I had a dream last night; I hope I never have another like it.

Freya had a real talent for drawing and wanted to improve her skill.

5–6 **Underline the adjectives.**

The old farmer drove the red tractor along the bumpy field.

The warm sun shone brightly on the sparkling sea.

7–8 **Underline the adjectival phrase.**

Our house, with the red front door, is next to the post office.

The centre of town, with its many narrow alleys, is easy to get lost in.

9 **Turn this direct speech into indirect speech.**
"You all need to beat the eggs well," the chef said to the cooks.

_____

10 **Use a subordinating conjunction in this sentence so that it makes sense.**

_____ we were hungry, we didn't eat all of the cake.

11–12 **Set out this speech, putting each person's new speech on a new line.**

"My name is Vijay," the little boy said, looking around at the other boys in the hall. "Welcome!" said the kind-looking leader. "I am sure that you will enjoy Cubs."

_____

_____

_____

_____

_____

12

Unit 10 Bond SATs Skills Grammar and Punctuation 8–9

13–14 Turn these questions into statements.

Is Joe upstairs in his bedroom?

_____

Shall I put the kettle on for a cup of tea?

_____

15–16 Underline 'has' or 'have' so that the sentences make sense.

The litter of kittens (has/have) been sleeping in the spare bedroom.

The daffodils (has/have) flowered late this year.

17–18 Write out the sentence replacing the underlined nouns with pronouns.

Mr Massoud showed Akeem and Bedar around his new house.

_____

_____

The mechanics worked hard all morning and the mechanics stopped for lunch at midday.

_____

_____

19–20 Underline the correct verb.

Rachel (sing/sings) in the girls' choir.

They will be (performed/performing) in the school concert.

21–22 Underline the adverbs in this sentence.

We carefully copied out the notes before quickly leaving the room.

Danny ran steadily around the track and successfully reached the finish line.

23–24 Add 'er' to the end of each verb to make a noun.

sprint _____

climb _____

Bond SATs Skills Grammar and Punctuation 8–9 **Unit 10**

25–28 Add adverbs to these sentences by adding 'ly' to the adjectives in capitals.

(SLY) The fox sneaked _____ into the chicken pen.

(JOINT) Delilah and Finn were _____ responsible for the mess in the classroom.

(BRISK) Amelia and Nadia walked _____ along the path through the wood.

(CLEAR) As the fog lifted, Ai was able to see the road ahead more _____.

29–46 Copy out the paragraph, adding capital letters and all punctuation.

we are going to the seaside said dad ive packed a picnic and got your swimming costumes called mum as we ran upstairs to find our buckets spades inflatable dolphin and the beach balls dad laughed and went to load the car

_____
_____
_____
_____
_____
_____

47–50 Turn these questions into commands.

Please can you turn off the light?

_____

Could you please clean your teeth?

_____

Can you tell me where you put the keys?

_____

Please will you pay attention?

_____

Unit 10

51–56 Complete each sentence so that they all make sense.

A _____ joins clauses together.

Add a _____ at the end of every question.

When writing, use _____ to show speech.

Use _____ in a list to separate items.

To show that something belongs to someone, we use an _____,

and for single owner, we put it before the letter _____.

57 A word that describes a noun is an _____.

58 A word that describes a verb is an _____.

59 A word that replaces a noun is called a _____.

60 An _____ phrase is a group of words that describe a noun.

61 Add the letters 'ed' to a _____ verb to show that the action is in the past.

 Helpful Hint

The answers to all of these **questions** are in your book, so if you are unsure, look back and find the answer. Now you are ready to move on to the next level.

Key words

abstract noun abstract nouns often refer to ideas or feelings. Abstract nouns cannot be touched, seen or heard, for example *anger*, *beauty*, *health*

adjectival phrase a group of words that describe a noun

adjective a word that describes a noun

adverb a word that describes a verb

clause a simple sentence that can be joined to another clause by using a conjunction

collective noun collective nouns refer to groups of people or things

comma (,) commas are used to separate items in a list

command commands usually have a verb at the beginning of the sentence and can end in either a full stop or exclamation mark, for example *Stop that!*

common noun the name of an object, for example *book*, *apple*

conjunction conjunctions join two clauses together and can be placed at the beginning or middle of a sentence

contraction a shortened way of saying two words, where an apostrophe replaces the missed out letters, for example *is not – isn't*

coordinating conjunction a coordinating conjunction joins two clauses together to make one complete sentence. The coordinating conjunctions are: for, and, nor, but, or, yet, so

direct speech when someone's exact words are quoted, for example *"I love you"*

exclamations (!) use an exclamation mark to show that your writing is meant to be shocking, funny or angry

full stop (.) a punctuation mark that is used at the end of a sentence

indirect/reported speech when someone is describing what someone else has said without quoting them directly, for example *Jo said she is running a bit late*

inverted commas (" ") punctuation marks used when quoting direct speech

personal pronoun words that replace the name of a person, place or object. The personal pronouns are: he, her, him, I, it, me, she, they, them, us, we, you

plural a noun is 'plural' when it refers to more than one thing

possession (use of apostrophe) use an apostrophe to show when somebody owns something, for example *Graham owns a bicycle – Graham's bicycle*

possessive pronoun words that show ownership. The possessive pronouns are: her, hers, his, its, mine, my, our, ours, their, theirs, your, yours, whose

pronoun a pronoun is used in place of a noun

proper noun nouns that need a capital letter, such as names of people and places, days of the week and months of the year, titles and organisations

question questions usually begin with question words such as: how, what, why, where, when and who and always end with a question mark **(?)**

simple sentence a simple sentence has a verb and a noun and it can have adverbs and adjectives, but doesn't have a conjunction

singular a noun is 'singular' when it refers to one thing

statements a sentence that gives information clearly and usually ends in a full stop

subordinating conjunction a subordinating conjunction is used to join a clause that is not as important as the main clause. The subordinating conjunctions include: after, although, as, because, before, it, since, when, while

verb (irregular) if you cannot add 'ed' to the end of a verb, it is called an 'irregular verb'. You have to change the verb to show that the action is in the past

verb (regular) if you can add 'ed' to the end of a verb, it is called a 'regular verb'. Adding 'ed' shows us that the action is in the past

Progress chart

Bond SATs Skills Grammar and Punctuation 8–9

How did you do? Fill in your score below and shade in the corresponding boxes to compare your progress across the different tests and units.

	50%	100%
Unit 1, p3 Score: __ / 18		
Unit 1, p4 Score: __ / 18		
Unit 1, p5 Score: __ / 9		
Unit 1, p6 Score: __ / 10		
Unit 2, p7 Score: __ / 12		
Unit 2, p8 Score: __ / 22		
Unit 2, p9 Score: __ / 5		
Unit 2, p10 Score: __ / 13		
Unit 3, p11 Score: __ / 15		
Unit 3, p12 Score: __ / 18		
Unit 3, p13 Score: __ / 16		
Quick quiz, p14 Score: __ / 35		
Unit 4, p15 Score: __ / 14		
Unit 4, p16 Score: __ / 14		
Unit 4, p17 Score: __ / 20		
Unit 4, p18 Score: __ / 10		
Unit 5, p19 Score: __ / 10		
Unit 5, p20 Score: __ / 18		
Unit 5, p21 Score: __ / 13		
Unit 5, p22 Score: __ / 18		

	50%	100%
Unit 6, p27 Score: __ / 19		
Unit 6, p28 Score: __ / 14		
Unit 6, p29 Score: __ / 17		
Quick quiz, p30 Score: __ / 19		
Unit 7, p31 Score: __ / 18		
Unit 7, p32 Score: __ / 7		
Unit 7, p33 Score: __ / 24		
Unit 7, p34 Score: __ / 10		
Unit 8, p35 Score: __ / 6		
Unit 8, p36 Score: __ / 13		
Unit 8, p37 Score: __ / 19		
Unit 8, p38 Score: __ / 17		
Unit 9, p39 Score: __ / 12		
Unit 9, p40 Score: __ / 14		
Unit 9, p41 Score: __ / 11		
Unit 9, p42 Score: __ / 10		
Unit 10, p43 Score: __ / 12		
Unit 10, p44 Score: __ / 12		
Unit 10, p45 Score: __ / 26		
Unit 10, p46 Score: __ / 11		